## ABOUT THE AUTH(

James W. Hart, IV has been involved in the field of residential  ..
commercial real estate mortgage financing since 1987. Hart, previ-
ously licensed to engage in the sale of real estate in the State of Ohio,
has been directly involved in the origination of residential and commercial financing and has worked with residential and commercial mortgage lenders, large commercial mortgage banking firms and life
insurance companies for financing. Additionally, Hart has performed
consultation services to clients seeking to secure financing for consoli-
dation and business loans.

Hart is an honorably discharged veteran of the U.S. Army, graduate of
the University of Toledo and graduate of the Cleveland Institute of
Electronics. He is a member of the National Panel of Consumer
Arbitrators and the Council of Better Business Bureaus, Inc.

## DEDICATION

To God who gave me the idea and ability to write this book and the
enthusiasm to complete the task. To my lovely wife Jean for her
encouragement and commitment. To the team that helped make the
book a reality. The success of the book is owed to him who said:
"Commit thy works to the Lord and your thoughts will be established".
Proverbs 16:3

**Note:** For the sake of brevity and avoiding the awkwardness of the
repeated use of he/she and him/her, masculine pronouns are used
throughout the text. The author is well aware of the widespread and
increasing presence of women in all areas of business and modern
society. The masculine pronouns are used solely for the sake of clarity
and readability.

## PREFACE

The information presented in *Everything A Real Estate Agent Doesn't Want You To Know* and the other books of the *MONEY: THE RULES* series is based upon and written with several founding assumptions:

1) You are a nice person who lives a relatively simple life style.

2) You are not a real estate or finance professional.

3) You are not a political giant.

4) You have limited or no experience dealing with real estate agents, mortgage lenders and other industry related professionals.

5) People will take advantage of you, rip you off and abuse you if they see an opportunity to do so and get away with it.

Man is a natural predator. Early man would beat his fellow man with clubs for women, territory rights (property) and power. In our modern society the club has been replaced by money. Money, whether we like it or not, controls our society, our economy and our lives. No money = limited power. No money = limited freedom. No money = limited opportunity. Limited opportunity = limited ability to make money. While money isn't everything it is the major force which drives mankind. The pursuit of money motivates most of us to work and all material goods produced and services offered cost MONEY!

The question then becomes: If I have no money or I have a little money, how do I protect myself? What is the right financial decision to make? How do I invest my money correctly? If I have no money, how do I get money? Who can I trust and how do I know I can trust them? These are all good questions and the answer is simple enough: "KNOWLEDGE".

Specific knowledge regarding any matter increases your opportunities and ability to protect yourself regarding that matter. An abundance of specific and practical knowledge regarding any matter gives you POWER! Specific knowledge = Power. Power = Opportunity. Opportunity = Money. Through SPECIFIC KNOWLEDGE you will have the power to make rational and good decisions, to protect yourself, to see opportunity which may not be apparent to someone without your knowledge and use the opportunity to make MONEY!

Welcome to *MONEY: THE RULES* This book and each book of the series is designed to give you information you need to know regarding the topic of the book. This information will help you avoid being taken advantage of and hurt by other people. This information is bottom line and the things some people don't want you to know, because by not knowing this information they make more money off of you! Simple enough! This information will put a sword in your hand, a shield on your arm and a helmet upon your head. If we battle each other today for money, then it makes good sense to put on your ARMOR.

# TABLE OF CONTENTS/TOPIC PAGES

## TABLE OF CONTENTS (Continued)

# REAL ESTATE AS AN INVESTMENT

We have all seen the shows on TV claiming that you and I can become millionaires by investing in real estate; get-rich-quick schemes that are seldom more than a few very expensive cassettes, some workbooks and a lot of "pie-in-the-sky". These programs tell you that you can purchase real estate with "nothing down" and that you will be on your way to successful real estate investing within a short time following their simple success proven program. They are trying to sell you the dream of fast, easy money through cassettes and books. The dream doesn't materialize for most of us.

What they don't tell you is how tough it is to find a seller who will allow you to buy their property with no money down! We have a market full of buyers looking for stupid sellers who will sell their property for next to nothing and a market full of sellers who are looking for ignorant buyers who will pay more than they should for their property. Think about how much time is wasted in these ventures. Would you sell your property to someone who had no money? If you would, please write me with your proposal!

These same fast-buck marketeers also don't tell you that our banking crisis makes it nearly impossible to secure investment loans with less that 25% to 35% down payment on non-owner occupied (investment) property. Creative financing, incompetent bankers and people who don't pay their loans are factors that have all but eliminated the nothing down, creative financing that existed during the 80's. All things are possible but not all things are probable. The point of the conversation is that you should understand that all the "pie-in-the-sky" no-money-involved real estate investment techniques are not very practical. If you choose to pursue that course, good luck!


# PRACTICAL REAL ESTATE INVESTMENTS

Most of us either rent a home, own a home, live with friends or family, or, for the unfortunate few, do not have a home. The practical questions for most of us are:

1) "Should I rent or should I buy a house?"

2) "How do I buy a home, make a good investment and avoid being abused by everybody involved?"

3) "What do I need to know and where do I start?"

These are good questions and will provide answers that are thought provoking, practical and self protective.

# RENTING VS BUYING

There are many advantages to renting a home. Renting an apartment or house often provides a nicer living environment and a bigger 'bang for the buck' than if you were to buy a home with the same monthly payment. In most cases maintenance is provided by the landlord and you don't have to worry about fixing broken water heaters and the like. Most rental agreements are short term which gives you the freedom to move without being locked into a house which may or may not sell quickly. For some investment-wise people, there may be better investments for their dollars than putting the money into a home loan payment. There is usually less responsibility when renting and if you find yourself unemployed and unable to make the monthly payments the landlord will kick you out of your apartment rather than foreclosing on your house and/or forcing you into a bankruptcy.

There are also many advantages to buying a home. When you make your monthly payments they are applied to something of value to you and they do not go to your landlord. Each payment you make reduces your financial debt and allows you to eventually own your home free and clear. Owning a home gives you the freedom to be creative and to modify your environment and, if you find yourself unemployed and unable to make the monthly payments, a lender will work with you longer than a landlord to help you keep your home. Other advantages of owning real estate are: 1) You can build up equity in your home by paying down on the home loan. 2) The house can appreciate in value over time. 3) There are beneficial income tax write-offs associated with home ownership. 4) If you buy the property correctly you can step into the house with instant equity. There is also a certain pride involved with home ownership. The house can reflect you as an individual, your personality and your accomplishments. Owning a home, a little niche in the world, has been a common dream of mankind since we dwelled in caves.

## APPRECIATION AND DEPRECIATION

Real estate is one of your safest investments if you know what you're doing. Don't be fooled by anyone; real estate is not guaranteed to automatically appreciate (gain value over time). It is very possible for real estate to actually depreciate (lose value over time). Many things can affect appreciation and depreciation of a house. The employment market around your home can have a big impact on whether your house appreciates or depreciates. If jobs are plentiful and people are moving into the area, home prices will probably be higher. If your area has suffered lay-offs and high unemployment rates, home prices could be stable or lower than normal. If the local electric company builds a nuclear power plant next to your home, the value of the home most likely will drop like a rock. There are ways to minimize your risk of buying into a depreciating market and actually improving your chance of investing in stable and/or appreciating markets. This is a function of market geography and correct purchasing habits.

2

# MARKET GEOGRAPHY

The three most important words in real estate are location, location, location. When buying a house, the most important decisions you make are the location of the property, the quality of the home and the price of the property. Whether your home appreciates, depreciates or remains stable in price is largely dependent on the location of the house. People typically should look to purchase homes in good market areas that have the following characteristics:

- Neighborhoods are clean, well maintained and crime free.

- Homes are located within a good school system, near shopping centers, libraries, post offices and other needed resources.

- Homes have easy access to local roads and highway systems.

- Homes are within walking distance of bus lines and within a half-hour driving distance from other transportation outlets such as airports, trains and waterways.

If you are contemplating buying a home now or in the future, you need to ask yourself serious questions about the market geography you are thinking about investing in. You need to define one of the following for yourself:

- Am I buying a nice home in a good market area?

- Am I buying a nice home in a bad market area?

- Am I buying a bad home in a good market area?

- Am I buying a bad home in a bad market area?

There are two basic rules about bad market areas:

1) A bad house in a bad market is hard to sell.

2) No matter how nice a property may be, if it is a bad market area, it will remain a nice house in a bad market area. A large percentage of the population will never look at the house just because of its bad location and it will be hard to sell.

There are two basic rules about good market areas:

1) A good house in a good market sells faster and easier.

2) A bad house in a good market area can be fixed up and sold for a profit faster and easier.

You don't have to be a real estate professional to understand the value of this information. However, it is important to think about this information when looking at real estate. What is the state of the local economy? Do you see new housing projects being developed? What effect will that have on home sales? How are the job markets? What is the unemployment rate? Are new industries coming to the area you want to buy in? What are the future growth areas? These are important questions and if you want information about economic trends, contact your local chamber of commerce. Local government agencies like the planning commission, economic development councils and the like can provide information on real estate trends for you.

## THE HOUSING SUPPLY

Besides the traditional source of homes (real estate companies) there are other sources of homes including "For Sale By Owner" properties and bank repossessions. "For Sale By Owner" properties (commonly referred to as FSBO'S and pronounced fisbo's) can be found directly in the classified ads of your local newspapers or in specialty newspaper magazines commonly called "FOR SALE BY OWNER MAGAZINES". You can call the banks in your area (or the area you desire to live in) and ask for a list of repossessed homes that will be available for sale (or auction) now or in the near future. The FSBO market is the second largest (and growing) supply of homes for sale to the public. The first largest supply is still the listings offered by real estate companies that represent most of the homes that are for sale in the market place. There are advantages and disadvantages to working with both the FSBO and real estate companies.

## REAL ESTATE AGENTS VS. FOR SALE BY OWNER

The single biggest advantage to buying a FSBO property is that the buyer can purchase the home at a lower price because the seller does not have to pay the real estate commissions involved when the home is sold through a real estate company. Other than price there are not many other benefits involved. Sometimes, FSBO'S have their homes way overpriced and the asking price is based on the wrong reasoning. For example: The sellers have been in their home for 20 years, love their oak tree and don't really want to sell the home unless they get top-dollar for it. Do you want to waste your time on this deal? The other problem with limiting yourself to working strictly with FSBO'S is that you deny yourself the opportunity to have access to all the properties that are on the market, including the large share for sale through real estate companies. Typically, most people who are selling their own homes are not in a real rush to sell it. If you're buying a home, the last thing you need to deal with is an unmotivated seller. How can you negotiate the best price with a seller who is in no rush to sell?

The single biggest advantage to working with real estate companies is that you will have access to all the properties that are available for sale in a given area. Real estate companies share this property information through a computer network known as the "Multiple Listing Service". This program allows a real estate agent to key-in your desired property and market information and obtain a computer print-out list of properties that generally meet your specifications. Other than access to the properties in the marketplace, there are not many real benefits to working with a real estate company or Real estate agent. Real estate agents are basically middle-men who get paid a commission when you buy a house through them. Because there is a commission paid to the real estate company when you buy a house, the prices of the properties are often higher to cover these commissions.

# BUYING REAL ESTATE INTELLIGENTLY

The first rule of buying a home intelligently is to remember that BUYING A HOME SHOULD BE A BUSINESS DECISION. You will be the one who has to live in the property and make the payments. Too many home buyers, especially first time home-buyers, make the major mistake of buying a home while being carried away on an overwhelming whirlwind of emotion. Remember: everybody involved with a real estate transaction is selling, except you; you're buying. People sometimes sell themselves into a bad deal because they get carried way with emotion. DO NOT LET YOUR EMOTIONS CONTROL YOU; CONTROL YOUR EMOTIONS.

People who have little or no experience buying real estate typically call a real estate company, talk to a real estate agent (a sales person) who shows them properties until they find one closest to their "dream home". As soon as you, or your mate, shows the emotion called "WANT" to a real estate agent, you start to lose negotiating control and, possibly, your money. Remember: some of the real estate agents out their are professional sales people who know how to persuade you, manipulate you and "sell you" into doing something you don't really want to do. For those who have never been in a straight commission sales career before, you must realize that the most important thing to commissioned sales persons is their check, which in the real estate agent's case arrives only if he sells homes.

Purchasing real estate is an art and a science. There is a systematic approach to preparing yourself financially and mentally for the task of intelligent real estate purchasing. The goal is to WIN the negotiating process and get the seller to sell the home at the absolute best price while not letting anybody hurt you or cause you financial pain in the process. It has often been said (by sales people) that the best sale is one where everybody wins. This is commonly referred to as a "win-win" situation. The true winner in a win-win situation is the sales person because they get their check. I personally believe that a successful real estate deal is a win-lose situation. YOU WIN, they lose.

Now that we have touched on some common-sense aspects of real estate we need to focus our attention on the formula which allows you to win and WIN BIG in the negotiating game of real estate. To do this we need to understand some fundamentals of the real estate industry and learn the things real estate agents don't want you to know. You will discover that a few simple and practical insights will put you head and shoulders above the crowd when you are ready to begin looking for your home.

# UNDERSTANDING REAL ESTATE AGENTS

REAL ESTATE AGENTS REPRESENT SELLERS NOT BUYERS. A lot of people think that their friendly real estate agent is representing their best interest when they're out looking at real estate. This is absolutely not true. Real estate agents have a fiduciary (legal) relationship with the sellers of properties to bring to the seller a ready, willing and able buyer who will pay the maximum or best price for the home. How can that real estate agent represent your best interests when they represent the seller's best interest?

Even if your real estate agent is your mother, father, aunt, uncle, brother, sister, cousin or best friend, they have a legal duty to the seller of the house to sell you the house at the highest possible price. If you don't believe this statement, call a lawyer and ask them who the real estate agent is obligated to represent under the law. The only exception to this rule is if you retain a real estate agent, under contract, as a BUYER'S REPRESENTATIVE. If you decide to have a real estate agent represent you then you must be prepared to pay them the typical commission of around 7% of the selling price of the home. If you are working with a real estate agent who is acting as your representative and you buy a house through that real estate agent for $100,000.00 you would pay the real estate agent who is representing you $7,000.00 in commissions disregarding any other conditions. That is a lot of money for a real estate agent to show you a home! If you bought a home through your real estate representative, and that house was being sold by another real estate company, then you would not only pay your representative a commission, but, you would also pay an inflated price for the home to cover the cost of commissions the seller will pay the real estate company for selling the home! Talk about a double-dip deal!

REAL ESTATE AGENTS ARE SALES PEOPLE! Real estate agents work on straight commission. Real estate agents make money when they sell you a home. No sale = no check. Think about this statement and ask yourself what motivates the real estate agent: Finding you a home that is a good quality investment for you, or finding a home that you write the highest purchase offer on, as quickly as possible, so they can get their quickest, biggest check? What do you honestly think the most important thing to a real estate agent is? If you said "Their check" you are correct. Real estate agents will do and say just about anything to get you to do a deal with them. Besides representing the seller's best interest, real estate agents also represent their best interests...their financial interests!

CAVEAT EMPTOR. Every real estate person has heard this term during the training for their real estate license or at some point in their career and they won't share it with you. The statement means "BUYER BEWARE". It is your duty to "beware" of the property, the seller, the real estate agents and all parties involved with a real estate transaction. That is a tall order for the common person. You could buy a disaster of a house and have no legal way to get your money back! The whole real estate industry is designed, built and operated around the seller, not the buyer.

## UNDERSTANDING REAL ESTATE AGENTS

Not everyone in the real estate industry is a crook or will hurt you and cause you financial pain. However, a good, honest, knowledgeable, full-time, professional real estate agent, who is in the business to help you achieve your specific goals and objectives, make proper and sound investment decisions and help you purchase a home that meets your individual needs now and in the future, at the best possible price is nearly impossible to find!

The three most important rules to remember when working with real estate agents is: 1) Don't trust them. 2) Don't trust them. 3) Don't trust them. There are a few general things to remember about real estate agents:

You should be cautious of every real estate agent who you come in contact with. Don't trust them and don't take their word on anything. If it is a fact, get it in writing. Stay away from part-time real estate agents and only work with energetic professionals.

## NEW REAL ESTATE AGENTS

New real estate agents typically have limited knowledge, work full or part time and are fairly incompetent until they get a few deals under their belt. It makes sense to avoid doing business with a new real estate agent because they may or may not know what's going on or what's on the market. However, new agents are sometimes innocent enough not to hurt you on purpose.

## SEASONED REAL ESTATE AGENTS

Seasoned real estate agents typically have more experience in real estate than do their newer associates. However, that doesn't necessarily mean they are better. Real estate agents may work full or part time, and, nothing is worse than a part-time agent. Part-timers are usually not worth your time if you're buying or selling real estate. If you are going to spend time with a real estate agent, make sure he is full-time and works hard for a living.

## PROFESSIONAL REAL ESTATE AGENTS

Professional real estate agents work full-time, have a great degree of market knowledge and are very experienced with real estate transactions. These are the real estate agents you want to work with. However, be cautious! A professional real estate agent can sell sunglasses to a blind man!

The spectrum of realty agent personalities runs from retirees who have nothing better to do than to sit around real estate companies (and maybe will do a deal this year) to full-time professionals who can sell you anything. They know how to manipulate you, persuade you and make you do what they want you to do (buy real estate at the highest price). The honesty level of real estate agents ranges form 'very honest' on one hand to 'you know what' on the other hand. In summary, don't trust them and don't take their word on anything!

## HOW REAL ESTATE PEOPLE GET PAID

Real estate agents work for real estate companies who work for the seller. As was mentioned earlier, sellers pay the real estate company a commission of (typically) 7% of the selling price of the home when the property sells. There are two kinds of real estate agents and two kinds of real estate companies. Real estate agents and their companies can be either kind or both. I'll explain:

A real estate agent can only work for one company at a time. A real estate company can be either a listing company, selling company or both. A real estate agent can be a listing agent, selling agent or both.

When a homeowner decides to sell a house through a real estate company, the homeowner enters into a LISTING CONTRACT with a real estate agent and his/her company. This listing contract specifies that the real estate agent and the company have the right to sell the homeowner's house for a specified period of time. The home-owner agrees to pay a real estate commission of (typically) 7% of the selling price of the house to the company that "listed" their home for sale. Now, if the real estate agent that "listed the house for sale also sells the house, then that real estate agent is said to be the listing and selling agent. The agent's company would receive the full check of $7,000.00 and, for simplicity, the real estate company splits the money with the real estate agent so that the company makes $3,500.00 and the agent makes $3,500.00

Now, assume that there are two real estate companies called Company A and Company B and each company has a real estate agent working for them. The real estate agent for Company A listed the home-owner's property for sale with Company A. However, the real estate agent for Company B sold the property. As in the earlier example, if a real estate agent sells a $100,000.00 house, the Seller pays a real estate commission to the listing company (Company A) of $7,000.00 dollars. In this case, however, the commission of $7,000.00 paid to Company A gets split-up between company-A, the agent for Company A, Company B and the agent for Company B in the following simplified manner:

Total commission = $7,000.00 (100% of total). Commission Company-A = $3,500.00 (50% of total); Commission Company-B = $3,500.00 (50% of total); Balance = $0

Company-A total = $3,500.00, Company-B total = $3,500.00. Agents' commission (50% of total-A) = $1,750.00, (50% total-B) = $1,750.00. Company-A check = $1,750.00 Company-B check = $1,750.00

If you have any questions on how real estate agents get paid, feel free to call the local Board of Realtors™ for further explanation.

# HOW TO START BUYING REAL ESTATE

The absolute first rule to buying real estate (correctly) is to get your home financing together first. Doing so will save you hours of wasted time, heartache and money. There are two primary sources of home financing: BANKS and MORTGAGE COMPANIES. The difference between dealing with a loan officer from a bank and a mortgage company is that the banker gets a check on Friday whether the banker finances your home or not. On the other hand, loan officers for mortgage companies are paid a commission when you get your home loan and, therefore, have much greater incentive to work with you to secure your home financing. There are many things you should know about MORTGAGE LENDERS before you select one to secure your home financing. There are a number of crooked, up-front-fee lenders who will rip you off and not get your home loan for you. For this reason it is strongly recommended that you be very cautious when dealing with any mortgage lender and see at least three loan officers from different lending institutions before making a final decision on where to get your home financing. It is important to share with you some important basics that you need to know to start buying a home.

1)    Decide what you want your TOTAL house payment to be. This is the first and most important financial question you need to ask yourself. You are the one who will make the payments on the home. Be reasonable. Your total loan payment should not exceed 28% or 29% of your gross monthly income.

2)    Understand that your total house payment represents payment on the Principal loan amount, payment of Interest on the loan, real estate Taxes and home Insurance. These payments are combined into a single house payment known as your PITI payment (pronounced "pity payment"). This payment represented the TOTAL payment to the lender.

3)    Call the local mortgage bankers association in your area and ask for the names of three (3) good mortgage companies and/or banks. If there is no bankers association in your area, call some real estate companies in your area and ask for the names of three (3) known lenders. DO NOT GET INVOLVED WITH A REAL ESTATE AGENT YET!

4)    Meet with one loan officer from three (3) different lending institutions and ask them to explain the different conventional and governmental loan programs in your area that will meet your specific needs. Remember: loan officers and lenders are sales people. They're selling you money! Buyer Beware.

## HOW TO START BUYING REAL ESTATE

5)    Have the loan officers pre-qualify you for a home loan. Pre-qualification for a home loan costs you nothing or, at worst, a few dollars (no more than the cost of your credit report). A loan officer will be able to tell you if you are qualified for a home loan, how much you can borrow and how much cash you will need to complete the home purchase under the various loan programs. Find out about low down payment FHA loans, 15 and 30-year conventional loans, adjustable rate loans and VA loans if you're a veteran of the armed services.

6)    Once you understand the advantages and disadvantages of the various loan programs and have been pre-qualified by a loan officer you should select a lender you feel comfortable with and get the loan officer to give you a LETTER OF PRE-QUALIFICATION. This letter should clearly state the following information:

   a)  How much you are qualified to borrow.
   b)  What loan program you will be using.
   c)  The letter should be signed and dated by the loan officer on the lending institution's letterhead.

7)    The key here is to GET IT IN WRITING. As you will learn in the section on THE BASICS OF NEGOTIATIONS, having a pre-qualification letter in hand when you are looking at real estate gives you increased power. Power to make the real estate agents work hard, power to make the sellers negotiate. In fact, a letter of qualification gives you the same perceived power as a cash buyer when dealing with a seller! Talk about a negotiating tool! And it costs you nearly nothing!

8)    Other benefits to pre-qualification are that you know how much you can borrow, what your payments will be and you'll pick up a lot of knowledge about loan programs if you ask for the information. If you're not qualified to purchase a home at this time, at least you will know why. Ask the loan officer(s) what you must do to become qualified in the near future. Nobody wants to find out they can't buy a home. However, it is better to know right away than to waste your valuable time looking at property you can't afford to buy. I have seen real estate agents waste people's time showing them property again and again that they can't afford to buy. Getting pre-qualified saves you and everybody else involved a lost of wasted time if you can't get a home loan. You will get more free credit advice than you ever dreamed possible form loan officers of mortgage companies. Loan officers make money when you get a loan through them. No loan to you = No check to them. They want to show you how to improve your financial position so that you can come back to them in the future and be qualified for a home loan! I am sure this makes sense to you.

## SELECTING A REAL ESTATE AGENT

The first thing you should realize is that real estate agents are a dime a dozen. Look in the phone book under "real estate" and you'll see a number of real estate companies who have agents ready to sell you any property you want to buy or they can sell you. If you have come this far in the book you have more knowledge than most people who haven't (or have) dealt with a real estate agent before. The objective now is to select the right real east agent(s) to look for property for you. To complete this task we will discuss some basics and apply some fundamental logic to the real estate selection process.

RULE 1: Do not let family, friends or friends of the family sell you real estate. This might make you feel a little uncomfortable at first and it might make your friends and family mad for a while, but it is in your (and their) best interests not to buy real estate from them. Here's why: Nothing, and I mean nothing, can damage a personal relationship faster than a bad business deal. Family and friends might be angry that you didn't buy a home through them. But this is much better than the long-term damage and bad feelings associated with buying a home that turns out to be a bad deal in any way, shape or form. In addition, a real estate agent will learn something about your personal finances through the home purchase process. The last thing you may wish is to have a friend or family member know this information. What if you don't get a house because you have a credit problem or not enough money to complete the purchase? An unpleasant situation could arise, if at a party, your friend or family real estate agent has had a little too much to drink and accidently shares your personal (and maybe embarrassing) information with other family members. Trust this sound advice: Business is business and friends and family are friends and family. KEEP THEM SEPARATED! If a family member or friend does something wrong that costs you money, the damage is usually permanent. Steer away from this and keep your confidential information confidential.

RULE 2: Call the local BOARD OF REALTORS™ and ask them if there are any real estate companies that you should specifically avoid doing business with. You should ask for their opinion of the more professional, full service real estate companies in your area. Get the names of three (3) good real estate companies. If there is no local BOARD OF REALTORS™ where you live, call the Better Business Bureau, the local chamber of commerce or a few attorneys in town for references to good companies.

## SELECTING A REAL ESTATE AGENT

RULE 3: Drive around the areas in which you would like to purchase property. By now you should have been pre-qualified and know pretty much what you can afford to buy. As you drive around the desired area, look at the yard signs in front of the homes. Which real estate companies have signs on lawns in the area? Which company has the most signs on the lawns? What are the three (3) real estate company names that appear again and again? These are the real estate companies you should contact first.

RULE 4: Contact at least three (3) real estate companies and select (no more than) one (1) real estate agent from each company. The last thing you want is for the real estate agent to think that you are shopping them to death. Limit your selection to just one real estate agent per company. This way you will have multiple people working for you without crossing any wires within a single office.

RULE 5: You want three (3) or four (4) full-time real estate agents working for you at any one time. Why? Because not all real estate agents are hard-working, aggressive and keep track of all the property coming on the market for sale every day. Remember: Good properties at good prices are on the market for a matter of hours or days before they are sold. If you only have one (1) part-time real estate agent working for you and he is lazy, who will keep track of the good deals coming up for sale on the market for you? What if your real estate agent is sick the day the perfect deal for you comes up for sale and the property is sold without you ever knowing about it? You want as many feelers out there as possible. The more real estate agents you have looking for property for you, the greater your chances of finding a good property at a dynamic price. It does make good sense to be loyal to each real estate agent you have selected from each company as long as you are getting the service you deserve. If one of the real estate agents doesn't communicate and stay in touch, terminate the relationship with that agent and get a replacement.

RULE 6: SCREEN THE REAL ESTATE AGENT BEFORE YOU SELECT THEM TO LOOK FOR PROPERTY FOR YOU. On the next page you will find a real estate selection form designed to enable you to quickly determine if a real estate agent is professional enough to look for property for you. Make copies of this form for your personal use. Call the real estate companies and ask to speak to the sales manager. Ask the sales manger who his top full-time real estate agents are. You will want to deal with one (1) of these folks. If the sales manager is unavailable and you must talk to a real estate agent, USE THE FORM ON PAGE 13 and maintain control of your conversation with the real estate agent.

# MONEY, THE RULES
## EVERYTHING A REAL ESTATE AGENT DOESN'T WANT YOU TO KNOW
## REAL ESTATE AGENT SELECTION FORM

REAL ESTATE COMPANY NAME:_____

PHONE NUMBER:_____

SALES MANAGER:_____

HOW LONG HAS THE COMPANY BEEN IN BUSINESS?_____

HOW MANY AGENTS ARE IN YOUR COMPANY?_____

NAME OF TOP-3 FULL-TIME REALTORS: _____

_____ Home phone:_____ Agent A1
name (first and last)

_____ Home phone:_____ Agent A2
name (first and last)

_____ Home phone:_____ Agent A3
name (first and last)

| | A1 | A2 | A3 |
|---|---|---|---|
| How long have you been a real estate agent? | ___ | ___ | ___ |
| Are you full-time or part-time? | ___ | ___ | ___ |
| How many homes have you sold so far this year? | ___ | ___ | ___ |
| Do you have any professional designations in real estate? | ___ | ___ | ___ |
| Do you have three (3) references I can call that you sold to this year? If no, why not? | ___ | ___ | ___ |
| In which geographic areas are you most familiar with properties? | ___ | ___ | ___ |

I am going to select one (1) real estate agent from your office; can you tell me why I should select you over all others?

Agent-A1 _____

_____

Agent-A2 _____

_____

Agent-A3 _____

_____

\* You should contact the sales manager to verify the information provided to you by the real estate agent

# UNDERSTANDING THE HOME PURCHASE PROCESS

Purchasing a home intelligently requires a combination of things to occur in an orderly fashion, including getting pre-qualified for home financing, determining the price range of homes you will look at, selecting the real estate agent(s) you will be using to find property for you and analyzing various homes carefully before writing a purchase offer on the home you wish to purchase. When these ingredients are in place, you still have to control the real estate agent, negotiate the purchase price, write a purchase offer on the property, submit the offer to the seller, negotiate counter-offers and structure the deal so that you WIN while protecting yourself legally and financially.

In order to accomplish this result you need to know some basic real estate information which will make you far more knowledgeable than the average person (and some real estate people). It is important that you understand some basic real estate principles and practices of real estate, negotiations, the tactics real estate agents can use on you to manipulate you into paying too much for property and the techniques you can use to control the real estate agents. Your objective is to purchase the best property at the lowest possible price.

## NEGOTIATIONS

EVERYTHING IS NEGOTIABLE (except death and taxes). The key to negotiating the best possible real estate deal is to get your financing together first. If you don't know how much you can borrow or whether you can even get a home loan, than you have absolutely no foundation of strength from which to start negotiating with a seller. There are a few basic things you should know about negotiations and they are as follows:

## TIME

The one thing that we all have in common is that we go to the "time bank" every day and take out 24 hours whether we like it or not. We can't save time or make more time, we can only SPEND IT. All of us have been given 24 hours per day to spend in any way we choose. We can spend it wisely or we can waste it. Therefore, TIME is a PREMIUM. Your time and everybody else's time is very valuable whether we realize it or not. The point is that time has value. If a seller wants to sell his property quickly for whatever reason, then you, as a buyer, have more value (negotiating power) if you can help solve the seller's problem quickly. There is value in not wasting time. The bottom line to successful real estate negotiation is knowing that you have the power to borrow the money to buy real estate. Knowing how much you can borrow is your first strength.

## FIRST RULE OF REAL ESTATE NEGOTIATION

THE FIRST RULE OF STRATEGIC NEGOTIATIONS IS GET CONTROL. Get control of yourself, take control of the real estate agent and get control of the seller. THE FIRST RULE OF CONTROL IS KNOW YOUR STRENGTHS AND WEAKNESSES. Your primary strength when buying real estate should be your knowledge of how much money you can borrow. If you can borrow $50,000.00, and that is all you can borrow, then you know what your strength is (and also your weakness). But, at least YOU KNOW! Real estate agents are many things but they are not loan officers. You should not spend time with a real estate agent unless you are pre-qualified for a home loan and have a letter of pre-qualification indicating the amount of money you are qualified to borrow. A LETTER OF PRE-QUALIFICATION FROM A LENDER CAN HELP YOU SAVE THOUSANDS OF DOLLARS OFF THE SELLING PRICE OF A HOME! As I indicated earlier, the first rule of successful real estate negotiations is: FINANCING FIRST!

## STEP-NEGOTIATIONS

Understand this simple fact: Sellers have their properties priced higher than what they really need to in order to cover the costs of the commissions paid to the real estate agent. Keep in mind that when a seller sells his home the money from the sale of the house is broken down as follows:

> SELLING PRICE
> -REAL ESTATE AGENT'S COMMISSION
> = CASH PROCEEDS FROM SALE
> - PAY OFF EXISTING HOME LOANS (if any)
> = PROFIT TO SELLER

There is always room for negotiations in the selling price of a home—not hundreds of dollars, but THOUSANDS OF DOLLARS! Whenever you write a purchase offer on a home, you want your first offer to be at least 10 or 20% lower than the asking price of the property. Do not be afraid of insulting the seller! Understand that the seller has established a high asking price with room for negotiation built into the price! In every transaction where money is negotiable, one party starts HIGH and the other party starts LOW. The art of negotiation is finding the "real middle ground" of the deal. One way to determine a seller's price flexibility is to take note of the incremental changes in his counter-offers. Assuming a seller is asking $70,000.000 for his property and your first offer is $62,500.00 chances are the seller will make a counter-offer. It the seller counters with, say $68,500.00 then the seller has made a price concession of $1,500.00. That size price concession should indicate to you that the seller has more room for negotiation. You can tell how much room there is for negotiation by the incremental changes in the asking price. On the other hand, the seller can tell how bad you want the property by the size of the incremental changes of your counter-offers.

## STEP-NEGOTIATIONS

The point of step negotiations is that the seller has already established the upper price limit. You need to establish the lower price threshold. That is the HIGH and LOW part of the game of negotiations. If, as in the earlier example, the seller lowers the asking price from $70,000.00 to $68,500.00, you may want to raise your offer in increments of $500.00 rather than thousands. Small price changes indicate how close you are to the real price you will pay for the property or the real price the seller will sell the property for. The art of step negotiations is to know where to start the low threshold. A good rule of thumb is: MAKE YOUR FIRST OFFER 10% LESS THAN THE SELLING PRICE OF THE PROPERTY. Another good rule of thumb is: LOOK AT PROPERTY THAT COSTS FIVE THOUSAND TO SEVEN THOUSAND DOLLARS MORE THAN WHAT YOU ARE QUALIFIED TO BORROW. Why? Because you may negotiate the price down to the amount you are QUALIFIED TO BORROW! Remember: Everything is negotiable and you are the one who establishes the lower price floor. You want to watch the size of the seller's price change. If the change in asking price is large, that indicates there is more room for negotiations. If the change in the asking price is small, this could be an indictor that the seller is very close to the minimum selling price.

## POWER OF PRE-QUALIFICATION

As mentioned throughout the book, getting pre-qualified for home financing is the most important step in successful real estate negotiations. GETTING IT IN WRITING IS THE SECOND MOST IMPORTANT STEP YOU NEED TO TAKE!

One of the basics of negotiation is understanding that things in writing have more power than things that are not in writing. A letter of pre-qualification, on a lender's letterhead, gives you the same (perceived) power as a cash buyer. Cash buyers are able to negotiate outstanding deals in real estate because they have the power to satisfy the sellers want quickly by means of cash. Having the letter of pre-qualification in your hand accomplishes the same result. A seller is much more negotiable with a buyer if the buyer can give the seller what he wants quickly (cash). Remember, TIME IS A PREMIUM! A seller would much rather work with a buyer who has taken time to get pre-qualified and is ready, willing and able to buy the property now.

On page 17 you will find a sample letter of pre-qualification which you can copy for yourself and take to a lender as an example of what you want on paper. This letter is written so that the lender has no legal liability if you can't get a home loan for some reason. If you are qualified to buy real estate, a lender should give you a letter just like this one without any fees involved. You should, however think about securing your home loan from the helpful lender when it is time to do so.

1/2/91 .
ABC Mortgage Company
123 Jump Street
Highland, NJ 11001

To whom it may concern:

Please be advised that John and Mary Doe have pre-qualified for a home loan through ABC Mortgage Company on the_____ day of _____, 19____ . Our analysis indicates that the above mentioned party qualifies for a ( ) FHA ( ) Conventional mortgage loan through our company for an approximate amount of:

**$50,000.00**

1. This letter is valid four fourteen (14) days from the date signed by the loan officer

2. This letter does not guarantee financing for theentitled individual(s).

3. Financing and loan amounts are subject to property appraisals(s), inspections, verification(s), mortgage credit report(s) and final loan approval.

Loan Officer:                                   Client(s):


_____            _____
Loan Officer                                    Name

Date:_____            _____
                                                        Name

17

# HOW TO USE THE LETTER OF PRE-QUALIFICATION

Step 1:  Assume that you go to 2 or 3 banks or mortgage companies to discuss your financing and get pre-qualified for a home loan. After meeting with the loan officer(s), it is discovered that you have the ability to comfortably borrow a $50,000.00 home loan. Knowing this information, ask the loan officer to give you a letter of pre-qualification just like the one shown in the example on page 17. You want the letter of qualification because things in writing have more (perceived) power than spoken words. You need this letter to give you increased negotiating power. If possible, get the pre-qualification letter copied onto GOLD colored paper. Gold paper has a subliminal quality associated with money or monetary power. Having the letter of qualification on gold paper has greater emotional impact on the seller.

Step 2:  One you get the letter of pre-qualification, get a few (2 to 4) real estate agents looking for properties for you just like you learned earlier in the book. Except, here is the key:

Tell the real estate agent you are looking for properties in the $55,000.00 to $60,000.00 price range! If you have been pre-qualified in writing, always look at homes at least $5,000.00 more than what you are qualified to borrow!

Step 3:  When you find a house you are interested in, say in the $56,000.00 range, write your purchase offer for $50,000.00 and attach a copy of your pre-qualification letter to the purchase contract before submitting it to the seller!

Why? Because there is always a very good chance that the seller has had his property on the market for 180 days, has had 20 un-qualified people waste his time and mess up his carpeting and he has to deal with rookie real estate agents who want to show his property at all hours of the day. THE SELLER WANTS TO SELL HIS HOME! You know the price is inflated anyway to pay the real estate agent! What happens is this: You are forcing the seller to make a decision. The seller can accept your offer at $50,000.00 and sell his home today. Or, he can wait for another 25 un-qualified people to look at the house. Depending on the seller's need to sell, you just might get the offer accepted! If so, you save $6,000.00! If the seller doesn't negotiate, look at other properties! You will eventually find a seller who will come down in price when he sees the letter of pre-qualification attached to the purchase offer. The key here is: ASK NOT, RECEIVE NOT!

NOTE: Do not hesitate to be flexible with this purchasing technique. For more expensive properties, you want a larger spread between asking price and your first offer. For less expensive properties, you can expect a smaller spread between selling price and your first offer. Be shrewd when submitting your first offer on any property!

## MORE BENEFITS OF PRE-QUALIFYING

Besides being the most important step in the home purchase process, pre-qualifying has additional benefits including:

1)   A letter of pre-qualification is a competition killer.  If you and another party both are interested in buying the same home and you both write a purchase offer of equal value but you have a letter of qualification attached to your purchase offer, who's purchase offer do you think the seller will most likely accept?  Of course the seller will be much more interested in your purchase offer because you are prepared to buy his property.  The last thing the seller wants to do is to waste time waiting to find out if the other candidate can even get a home loan.  Again, time is a critical factor and a seller wants his money as fast as possible.

2)   Home financing is absolutely the most important part of the home purchase process. You are the one who will live with the house payments.  Getting pre-qualified first allows you time to think about the financial details of home ownership.  Most people spend their time looking at property, not knowing if they can buy a home or not, or, they get involved with a real estate agent who hustles them into buying a home quickly and, all of a sudden, the buyer has three business days to complete a loan application with a lender and make financial decisions that they will live with for a long, long time.  A good loan officer can explain home financing programs and answer any questions you may have about various home loans.  Home financing is the most important part of owning a home and you should fully understand what you are doing, why you are doing it and the advantages and disadvantages involved with the financing.

REMEMBER:  GET QUALIFIED, GET IT IN WRITING AND
MAKE YOUR FIRST BID ON A HOME 10% OR 20% LESS THAN THE ASKING PRICE

## UNDERSTANDING PURCHASE CONTRACTS

When you write a purchase offer on a home and the seller accepts that offer, you are involved in a purchase contract. A purchase contract is serious business and for this reason you should have a basic idea what they are and how to write them so that you can protect yourself.  The most important thing to know about writing a purchase contract is:  GET LEGAL ADVICE BEFORE YOU WRITE A PURCHASE OFFER.

# THE PURCHASE OFFER

After you have inspected a home for sale, you may want to write a purchase offer to buy the property. The purchase offer will contain the address of the property, your name and address, the amount of money you are offering to the seller as well as indicating the various financial information regarding your financing, down payment, etc. Most real estate companies require you to pay at least a $100.00 good faith cash deposit (called earnest money) when you submit your purchase offer on a property. That purchase offer must be delivered to the seller of the home as soon as possible (typically within 24 hours) from the time you submit the offer. If the seller accepts the offer you have a purchase offer contract between yourself and the seller in which you are legally obligated to live up to the requirements of the contract. The seller doesn't have to accept your offer and can either reject the offer or make a counter-offer.

There is no standard purchase offer. Purchase offers can contain any number of conditions. An important thing to know about purchase offers is that you can write them with release clauses that let you back out of the offer for any legitimate reason. In any contract there are conditions or clauses you can write in the contract that automatically release you from an otherwise binding contract. These release clauses are known as WEASEL WORDS. Weasel words are just what the name implies, they are phrases that can be written on a purchase contract that let you"weasel" out of the contract if the contract is not in your best interests.

THE MOST STANDARD WEASEL CLAUSE TO PUT IN A CONTRACT IS:

"SUBJECT TO ATTORNEY'S APPROVAL"

You can have a contract 50 pages thick, but if you write "subject to attorney's approval" anywhere close to and above your signature before you sign the contract, that contract is not binding on you until your attorney reads and approves the contract. If your attorney feels that the contract is not in your best interests and does not approve it, you are released from the contract!

## PURCHASE CONTRACTS—CLAUSES TO CONSIDER

Careful thinking should be given to writing a purchase offer on a home. Your goal is to purchase the best house at the best possible price and avoid being ripped off. Whenever you are buying a house you will likely find yourself negotiating the price of the home, what stays in the home, who pays closing costs for the home loan, when you will take over the house, etc. Below are several clauses that you can write in a purchase offer prior to submitting it to the seller. You can use any one clause or combination of clauses you choose and you should not hesitate to use at least one to protect yourself legally.

This contract will be binding on the buyer and seller subject to:

1) Buyer's Attorney's approval.

2) Professional home inspection satisfactory to buyer

3) Buyer able to secure home financing acceptable to buyer.

4) Seller produces marketable title acceptable to buyer.

## THINGS YOU SHOULD KNOW ABOUT PURCHASE CONTRACTS

As stated earlier, purchase offers are serious business. When the purchase offer is accepted by the seller of the property you have a legally binding agreement between you and the seller. If you do not perform your obligations the seller may have legal recourse against you for damages. If the purchase contract is not written correctly or you are guilty of non-performance under the purchase contract, the real estate agent and seller can keep your good faith deposit at best and bring legal action against you at worst. For that reason it is wise to talk to a lawyer before writing your offer or, at least, have a release clause written in the purchase offer.

You should realize that once the seller accepts your purchase offer, the seller is as legally obligated to perform under the purchase contract as you are. People may change their minds or think of something else they want after the purchase offer is written. Once the offer is accepted there is very little you can do to change the terms of the sale without mutual agreement between you and the seller. Also be aware that all real estate agents have a legal duty to deliver any legitimate purchase offer to the seller within a reasonable period of time. Do not be fooled. Even a very low offer must be delivered to a seller by the real estate agent so that the seller can make a decision regarding the offer. If a real estate agent doesn't present your offer to the seller within a reasonable period of time, he may be in violation of the law. Last but not least, make sure you pay your good faith deposit with a check or money order so that you have additional record of payment of the earnest money. Make sure that the purchase offer indicates the amount of money paid as good faith. The purchase offer will serve as additional proof of your payment.

# BUYER BEWARE—GAMES REAL ESTATE AGENTS PLAY

Never forget that real estate agents are sales people. Their major objective is to sell you a home at the highest possible price. The bigger the selling price, the bigger their check. When you are looking at houses for sale with a real estate agent, you should be aware of the subtle tactics a real estate agent may use against you to get you to buy a home. Sales people who "know how to sell" use a variety of sales techniques to persuade and manipulate you into buying something you may or may not want to buy. The objective of any sales person is to get you to say "yes" as many times as they can in a conversation with you. Why? Because every time you say "yes" you have agreed with them on a particular selling point and you are making minor commitments to them and yourself. The art of selling is a very complex talent, but the overall objective of a sales person is ask you questions so that you agree with them again and again. After you agree so many times regarding how you would benefit from the features of their product, when they ask you to buy the product, you feel like you have to buy it because you have agreed throughout the whole selling process that the product will benefit you! Professional selling is not a guessing game! It is a scientific system!

There are two principal tactics that can be used on you when a real estate agent is trying to sell you a house. They are TIE-DOWN STATEMENTS and PRESSURE TACTICS. These sales techniques are used to persuade you and manipulate you.

This is explained further because it is important with respect to controlling real estate agents who are trying to "sell you a house".

## TIE-DOWN STATEMENTS

So how does the sales person (real estate agent) get you to agree with him and say yes again and again? Let's examine a few words called TIE-DOWN WORDS and you will understand the concept:

Aren't you?  Shouldn't you?
Isn't it? Couldn't you?
Wasn't it?  Wouldn't you?
Can't you?  Could you?
Would you?  Weren't you?

These statements are always put at the beginning or end of a sentence so that you say "yes" as a natural response! Examples are given below.

## FAMOUS ONE LINERS

1)  If I can show you a nice home in a good location at a great price, you would take the time to look at it WOULDN'T YOU? Answer = yes. (Everybody is looking for a deal!)

2)  CAN'T YOU imagine yourself living in this home? Answer = yes. (Of course you can imagine living there!)

3)  You do want to buy a good home DON'T YOU? answer = yes. (Everybody wants to buy a good home!)

4)  We are going to go out and look at five houses that are just what you are looking for. You will write a purchase offer on one of these homes WON'T YOU? (you may not see any homes with this real estate agent if you say no!)

Always be on the look-out for these tie-down statements. you can find yourself agreeing so many times that you will feel STUPID if you don't buy the home. Don't ever buy anything because some hustler makes you feel guilty for not buying a property even after you have agreed over and over again that it was a great property!

## PRESSURE TACTICS

Unlike other sales people, real estate agents have special games they can play to get you to write higher purchase offers on property. Real estate agents can play mind-games with you and you don't even know you're being manipulated! I call these "mind-games" PRESSURE TACTICS (PT'S) and they may be used when you are ready to or have submitted a purchase offer on a home. Assume you are interested in writing a purchase offer on a home:

PT1   Somebody else has looked at this property twice, if you want to get this house you better act fast, write a good offer and tie up this property now before they buy it!

PT2   We just got a call from a real estate agent, they have a customer who wrote an offer on the home. I can call the seller and tell them you will write a higher offer. Better write it now before the seller accepts the other offer!

PT3   Your offer is way too low. I couldn't insult the seller with this offer. If you want this house, write a good offer that I can take to the seller

Assume you own a home now and want to write a purchase offer on another property:

PT4   I'm sorry, we won't look at your purchase offer unless you list your present house for sale with a real estate agent (himself, he is hoping).

Assume you have submitted a purchase offer on a home:

PT5 We just got a call from a real estate agent who has a customer who wrote a higher offer than yours. The seller knows your offer came in first and they will give you the opportunity to write a higher offer before they accept. If you want the property you better write a better offer fast.

## DEALING WITH PRESSURE TACTICS

You have to understand that these pressure tactics are out of your control. There may not even be another offer on the home! Because you can't see what is going on behind the scenes, you can be manipulated into paying more than you should on the property! Real estate agents may play these games with customers. Don't hit the panic button if this tactic is used against you. Always remember that there are a lot more homes available for sale than there are qualified buyers at any one time. If you find yourself being manipulated like this, take the real estate agent to the side and tell him that you don't care about the house enough to raise your offer any higher. That will get his attention! If the real estate agent is the selling real estate agent and not the listing real estate agent, he won't get a check if you don't buy the property. There may very well be a better offer on the property and you should be prepared to lose the opportunity to get the home if that is truly the case. However, if you wait for a few days, you'll be surprised at what you might hear about "the other person" who had the better offer that never came through!

## MORE GAMES REAL ESTATE AGENTS PLAY

Most buyers are not great business people and real estate agents know it! Inexperienced people make the mistake of believing everything a real estate agent tells them. The biggest mistake people make is not asking enough questions about the property, the sellers and the real estate agent's background and not getting the facts. The three most important rules to remember when working with real estate agents are:

1) Don't trust them.

2) Don't trust them.

3) Don't trust them.

Never take their word on anything!

# STEERING

Steering is a term used to describe the action of a real estate agent repeatedly showing you properties in certain neighborhoods that they feel are more "suitable" for you because of your race, creed, color or religious beliefs. Steering is a form of discrimination and it is illegal. Real estate agents who steer you into specific neighborhoods may be in serious violation of the law. Just because it is illegal to discriminate doesn't mean that it isn't done. If you find that a real estate agent is leading you to buy property in certain areas and you feel like you are being discriminated against, you can call your local Fair Housing organization and file a complaint against that real estate agent. Do not confuse this with the fact that lower price property is often located in less desirable neighborhoods. There is a difference between steering and showing you property that you can afford to buy. In other words, don't abuse the fair housing system. However, if you feel you have been or are being discriminated against, by all means use the fair housing system to solve the problem. You can also call the local Board of Realtors™ to file a complaint against the offending real estate agent.

## THINGS A REAL ESTATE AGENT MAY NOT WANT YOU TO KNOW

Keep in mind that real estate agents are usually aware of properties for sale where people are divorcing or are having severe financial problems and need to sell their properties. You may be able to buy a property for rock-bottom price if you know this information. Real estate agents represent the seller's best interests and may not share this information with you voluntarily. Even if you ask for this information, you may not get the details. In the same way, there may be problems with the property that a real estate agent is aware of, but "forgets" to tell you about or doesn't disclose to you at all. It is reasonable to assume that a real estate agent may not tell you all the problems wrong with a home if it makes the difference between your buying the property or not. Remember: Real estate agents represent sellers, not buyers.

## BEFORE YOU LOOK AT HOMES FOR SALE

Before you start looking at homes for sale you should decide what areas you would like to live in. It makes sense to pick 2 or 3 general locations where you would like to live before you begin house hunting. You also want to define the features you want and need in a home. You should be pre-qualified for home financing, and no matter how much you are qualified to borrow you want to look at property priced at least $5,000.00 more than what you are qualified to borrow. Why? Because you're not qualified to go up in price and that means the seller must come down in price. This can work like magic because you will find many sellers will come down at least $5,000.00 form the original asking price when your letter of qualification is attached to your purchase offer.

Before you start contacting real estate agents and looking at homes, remember this: Don't blindly trust anybody. It is safer to assume that everybody is out to get your money (and be wrong) than it is to think that everybody is looking out for your best interests (and be wrong).

## LOOKING AT PROPERTY

There is a difference between looking at property with a real estate agent and intelligently analyzing property before you buy it through a real estate agent. Looking at a home is much like looking at a gift-wrapped box. You can only guess what is on the inside until you are able to open it and take a good look at the contents. We are going to explore the basics involved in analyzing a home prior to writing a purchase offer. Further, we will explain how to control a real estate agent to help make sure you are getting the home you think you are buying.

Whenever you are working with a real estate agent and looking at property, ASK QUESTIONS AND TAKE NOTES! There is no such thing as a stupid question. You want to know as much as possible about the sellers, their reasons for selling, if they have financial problems, what the condition of the property is including plumbing, electrical systems, heating and ventilation systems, exterior condition (including the roof). Find out from the real estate agent what the properties around the houses you are looking at sold for during the past year or so and ask them to put it in writing on their company letterhead! IF A REAL ESTATE AGENT TELLS YOU SOMETHING ABOUT A HOME AND IT IS A FACT, GET IT IN WRITING!

## REAL ESTATE AGENT BEWARE—GAMES BUYERS CAN PLAY

On pages 28 and 29 you will find an IN-FIELD HOME ANALYSIS FORM. Feel free to make copies of this form for your personal use and take several copies of the form with you whenever you are looking at homes with a real estate agent. This analysis form is different from any you have ever seen before because, at the bottom of the form is a disclosure statement from the real estate agent to you which warrants that the real estate agent has told you the truth, the whole truth and nothing but the truth with respect to the subject property you are analyzing for possible purchase. If the real estate agent doesn't want to sign this form, a BIG RED FLAG SHOULD GO UP which indicates to you that the real estate agent is being less than truthful with you about what they know about the property. There is no liability to the real estate agent so long as the real estate agent is telling you all they know about the property. If, however, the real estate agent is aware of a major problem and doesn't share it with you, you may have legal recourse against the real estate agent.

## PROFESSIONAL HOME INSPECTIONS

It is in your best interests to higher a certified, professional home inspector to analyze a property you are very seriously considering for purchase. Home inspectors work for you, not the real estate agent or seller. It is your best source for a professional opinion regarding the structural soundness of a home. A good home inspector can find problems with a property before you write a purchase offer (or after the offer is accepted by the seller if you have a release clause in the purchase offer indicating that the offer is subject to professional home inspection acceptable to buyer). If there are major hidden problems with the home that are found by the home inspector, you can either get out of the deal (with a correct purchase offer) or negotiate a lower selling price to compensate for the repairs that may be required. In any case, it is best to have the property inspected by a professional. Most home inspections cost between $100 and $500.

## FREE ROOF INSPECTIONS

It is a well-kept secret that a buyer can call various roofing companies and ask for a free roof inspection on a home he is planning to buy. Roofing companies may send out one or two roofers to climb on the roof and render an opinion regarding whether the roof is in need of immediate repair or not. Many times the roof may require repair in the near future. You want to know this information before you buy the home, not afterwards! Roofers are more than happy to offer written estimates for the cost of repair because they might get a roofing job for the free estimate. It makes good sense to get at least two (2) opinions. If it is free you should take advantage of the service.

# IN-FIELD HOME ANALYSIS FORM

## General Information

Property address:_____         Asking price $_____

_____         How long on market?_____

_____         Owner's name:_____

_____         Owner's phone: _____

**Selling Agent:** _____        Home phone:_____

Company Name:_____         Work phone: _____

**Listing Agent:** _____        Home phone: _____

Company Name: _____          Work phone:_____

## Structural Checklist

| Item | Inspected | Condition | Comments |
|------|-----------|-----------|----------|
| Foundation | ☐ | _____ | _____ |
| Brick Work | ☐ | _____ | _____ |
| Exterior Finish | ☐ | _____ | _____ |
| Roof and Gutter | ☐ | _____ | _____ |
| Chimney | ☐ | _____ | _____ |
| Sidewalks/driveway | ☐ | _____ | _____ |
| Garage | ☐ | _____ | _____ |
| Fencing | ☐ | _____ | _____ |
| Porches | ☐ | _____ | _____ |
| Porch/steps | ☐ | _____ | _____ |
| Door entrance | ☐ | _____ | _____ |
| Windows (in/out) | ☐ | _____ | _____ |
| Walls/ceilings | ☐ | _____ | _____ |
| Floors/stairs | ☐ | _____ | _____ |
| Basement/attic | ☐ | _____ | _____ |

## Major Electro-Mechanical Systems

| Item | Inspected | Condition | Comments |
|------|-----------|-----------|----------|
| Electrical | ☐ | _____ | _____ |
| Plumbing | ☐ | _____ | _____ |
| Heating | ☐ | _____ | _____ |
| Water heater | ☐ | _____ | _____ |
| Air condition | ☐ | _____ | _____ |
| Floor Plan | ☐ | _____ | _____ |

## Features

☐ Family room    ☐ Garage    ☐ Large yard    ☐ Pool

☐ Fireplace    ☐ Jaccuzi/spa    ☐ Storage    ☐ Formal dining

☐ Laundry    ☐ Office    ☐ Workshop    ☐ Expandable

☐ Other:_____

☐ Any problems with property?_____

_____

☐ Notes_____

_____

The customer is relying on statements made by the undersigned Real Estate Agent in consideration of a potential purchase of the above referenced property. Therefore, Real Estate Agent hereby states to Customer that Real Estate Agent has fully disclosed all the information that Real Estate Agent knows regarding the above referenced seller and property.

_____    _____

Real Estate Agent    Date

_____    _____

Customer    Date

# THINGS REAL ESTATE AGENTS DON'T WANT SELLERS TO KNOW

If you are thinking of selling your home now or in the near future, you should be aware of some basic information that will help you decide between selling your home on your own or using the services of a real estate company to sell the home for you. The information will help you protect your interests when working with real estate agents or home buyers.

## SELLING YOUR OWN PROPERTY

You don't need a real estate agent to sell your home for you. There are many home-owners who successfully sell their own home through the various FOR SALE BY OWNER newspapers on the market. Selling your own home does require you to be available to answer phone inquiries and show your home to potential customers for a possible sale. This kind of sales activity can be both time-consuming and frustrating. However, if you are prepared to perform these simple selling requirements it may well be worth your time to sell your property "For Sale By Owner":

The three biggest mistakes self-selling owners make are as follows:

1) They overprice the property.

2) They talk too much and ruin potential sales.

3) They don't pre-qualify the customers before accepting the purchase contract.

## PRICING PROPERTY

It is widely known that you can call real estate companies and get a real estate agent to come to the home to give you a FREE MARKET ESTIMATE. A free market estimate is conducted by a given real estate agent in an attempt to get you to list the home for sale with him. The free market estimate is a sales gimmick real estate agents use to meet you and try to sell you on their company and services. Market estimates may be fairly accurate if the real estate agents performing the analysis is experienced and knowledgeable of property sales around your area. Like everything else, it is wise to have two or three opinions from real estate agents from different companies and have a few real estate agents come to your home to perform this FREE SERVICE! When you have two or three quotes from different real estate agents, that will give you a good idea what your home should sell for. Be aware, however, that real estate agents commissions may be built into the price quote. After they give you the free information, sell the property yourself using the information you gained from the real estate agents! If it is free, take advantage of it!

## QUALIFIED BUYERS

Whether you are selling your own home or working with a real estate agent, do not accept purchase offers from anybody unless you are absolutely sure they are qualified to purchase your home. When you accept a purchase offer, your property is effectively off the market. If you tie up your property with an unqualified buyer, you can wait up to 30 or more days before you find out the buyer is unqualified to get home financing. The last thing you want to find out after you have accepted an offer and had your property off the market for 30 days is that the BUYER IS NOT QUALIFIED TO BUY THE HOME! When you take your home off the market for an unqualified buyer, you lose the opportunity to sell the home to people who are qualified to purchase! For this reason, it makes good sense to request that a customer is pre-qualified for a home loan by a bank or mortgage company before entering into a purchase contract with a customer. Don't be fooled by people who "look like they could buy the home." Many attractive people with nice clothes and nice cars can't afford to buy a home because they spend all their money on nice clothes and fancy cars! MAKE SURE THE BUYER IS QUALIFIED TO BUY! One way to protect yourself is to get the name and phone number of the loan officer of the lending institution where the customer is going to be obtaining their home loan. You want the loan officer's opinion of the feasibility of the customer getting a home loan and you want to hear the information directly from the loan officer handling the loan!

One last comment on selling your own home: DON'T TALK TOO MUCH! One way to ruin a potential deal is to spend all your time talking when you should be listening. Buying a home is a big investment for most people and if somebody is going to buy your home, they will do so because they like the property and not because you "talk them into it." Talking too much about all the wonderful aspects of your home is overkill. Nothing that is too good to be true is true. Honesty is the best policy. Answer people's questions truthfully and without hype. If they want to buy the home, they will do so because they like the property and you are honest with them.

## SELLER BEWARE—GAMES REAL ESTATE AGENTS PLAY

If you decide, for whatever reason, that you want to sell your home through a real estate company, there are some things you should know about your relationship with the real estate agent who lists your home for sale and ways to protect your legal and financial interests before and during the selling process.

## REAL ESTATE AGENTS—IF THEY DON'T LIST, THEY DON'T LAST

It is common knowledge among real estate people that it is far easier (and more lucrative) to list property for sale than to actually sell the property to individual buyers. The main goal of the average real estate agent is to get as many listing agreements with home sellers as possible. Why? Because a listing agent doesn't have to actually sell the property for a home-owner in order to get paid a commission when the house sells during the contract period. Any real estate agent can sell your property and the listing agent will get paid at least half (and sometimes the greater percentage) of the commission check for the sale of your home! That means a real estate agent doesn't have to do any actual selling activity for you in order to get their commission check! Given this information, do you think a real estate agent is more interested in getting your listing agreement, doing very little selling work and hoping another real estate agent sells the property during the contract period or, actually trying to sell the house to individual buyers, one on one, and working very hard to sell your home? Real estate agents want as many listings as possible because this builds up their inventory of "homes for sale." The more homes real estate agents have in their inventory, the greater the chances that somebody else will sell one of the homes! Most successful real estate agents spend their time "listing" and less time "selling" real estate. Do you want a real estate agent to represent you and your home if he doesn't spend his time selling? IF YOU LET A REAL ESTATE AGENT LIST YOUR PROPERTY FOR SALE, YOU WANT THAT REAL ESTATE AGENT TO SELL, SELL, SELL!

Real estate agents live and die for listing agreements. Do you think it is reasonable that a real estate agent would tell you just about anything to get you to list your property with him? Any real estate agent can list your house for sale. Does it make sense to give your listing to a lazy person who wants (and hopes) somebody will sell your property for him (and you)? Of course not! Practical insight will reveal steps you can take to increase your chances of getting a good real estate agent to list your property for sale—one that works hard for a living by SELLING HIS LISTINGS!

## THINGS LISTING AGENTS DON'T WANT YOU TO KNOW

If you want to have some fun, call 2 or 3 real estate companies and tell them you are planning on listing your home for sale with a real estate agent. If a real estate agent answers the phone, you can pretty much bet that the friendly real estate agent will immediately offer his services! Most real estate agents will give you a nice, flowery presentation on why he and his company are the best company to sell your home. He most probably will give you facts and figures about all the property he has listed and sold and he will request an appointment to meet with you at your home (for a free market estimate). Realize that when the real estate agent comes to your home, chances are fairly certain he has a listing contract lurking somewhere in his briefcase! The primary objective is to get you to sign the listing contract with him! The point is, almost all real estate agents want your listing agreement (especially if you have a nice home that will sell easily). If every real estate agent wants your listing agreement and only a small minority of those real estate agents are full-time, professional sales people who have the experience, contacts and "ability to sell" your home, then, YOUR OBJECTIVE IS TO FIND THE REAL ESTATE AGENT WHO PRODUCES THE RESULTS.

There is a big difference between image and sales. You should not pick a listing real estate agent just because he is friendly, well-dressed and/or drives a nice car. You should pick a real estate agent to list your home who has a proven business and personal track record of successful real estate sales. Do you want a part-time real estate agent working for you? Do you go to a part-time doctor? Do you hire part-time lawyers? Of course not! You go to full-time professionals who are actively engaged in up-to-date, day-to-day business activities of their specialization. YOU ARE THE EMPLOYER. You are the one who will pay the real estate agent a commission when the home sells. Therefore, you should interview and select a real estate agent as carefully as you would hire an employee in business. Remember: Selling your home is a business transaction!

The nicer the property, the more you can negotiate with a real estate agent. The more your property is worth, the more you can negotiate with a real estate agent. If you have a good property in a nice location, your home will be easier to sell then a poor property in a bad location. Therefore, common sense should dictate how you treat real estate agents. Some property is so bad that a seller is lucky to get a real estate agent to take the listing at all and you should not lose perspective of this fact. You don't want to play hard-ball with a real estate agent if you don't have a property to back you up. Obviously, if you are selling a $1,000,000.00 mansion you can have a bad attitude if you want to! Otherwise, be as pleasant as possible with real estate agents and keep in mind that there are good and bad in any business.

## REAL ESTATE AGENTS BEWARE—GAMES SELLERS CAN PLAY

The objective of a seller is to sell property at the highest price as quickly as possible. If you are going to sell your home, you want a good real estate agent representing you to make sure your interests are protected. Listing contracts are serious business. Therefore, it is strongly suggested that you retain the services of an attorney to review the listing contract prior to signing it with a real estate agent or, at least, make the agreement subject to your attorney's approval.

## HOW TO SELECT A LISTING REAL ESTATE AGENT

Before interviewing any real estate agent for a potential listing, call at least three real estate companies and talk to the sales manager. ASK THE SALES MANAGER FOR THE NAMES OF THE TOP THREE, FULL-TIME REAL ESTATE AGENTS WHO ARE SALES LEADERS IN YOUR AREA. The sales manager can easily provide you with the names and phone numbers for personal contact. Then, call the real estate agents and use the REAL ESTATE AGENT SELECTION FORM when you are talking to them. The real estate agent selection form will help you ask the appropriate interviewing questions and provide a record for review. After talking to the various real estate agents, you want to set an appointment at your home so they can see your property and make their presentations before you make your final selection and award the listing agreement (or decide to sell the property on your own!)

## NEGOTIATING THE LISTING AGREEMENT

Listing agreements are not written in stone and can be negotiated. Following is a brief discussion on various aspects of the listing agreement and points that can be negotiated.

## COMMISSIONS

Real estate commissions normally range between 5% and 7% of the selling price of the home. Depending on the quality of your property, you will want to attempt to negotiate the commission downward toward 5%. If you have a good property in a good market that will sell easily, the real estate agent won't have to put as much time into the sale of your home. Therefore, you have the right to attempt to negotiate the commission. You might offer to pay a 5% commission plus a bonus to the selling real estate agent if the house is sold within a desired (and specified) period of time. If a real estate agent will not negotiate the commissions with you, you may want to interview a few more real estate agents and see what kind of feedback you get from them regarding the commission. Everything is negotiable.

# PERFORMANCE AGREEMENTS

Avoid entering into a long-term listing contract with a real estate agent. The last thing you want to do is to sign a long-term listing agreement with a real estate agent and real estate company that can't sell your home. Instead, negotiate a 90-day listing agreement. This will give them a greater sense of urgency to sell your home quickly! After 90 days, if they haven't sold the property, consider extending the agreement in 30 day increments. If, after 120 days, the real estate agent hasn't sold your home, you may want to consider finding another real estate agent. If a real estate agent refuses to give you a short-term listing agreement, call other real estate agents to see if this is common practice in your area. The benefit of a short-term listing agreement is that it gives you the opportunity to review the performance of the listing real estate agent and his company. In this way, you can terminate the listing agreement if you find yourself doing business with a non-producing real estate agent.

# MINIMUM PERFORMANCE

You can negotiate in the listing contract, or in an addendum to the listing contract, a guarantee of how many open houses the real estate agent will hold for you within the time frame of your listing contract. The real estate agent should make selling your house a first priority. That means he will have at least one open house per month and show your home at least once a week. If you never see the real estate agent, the open houses don't happen and nobody looks at your property, consider terminating the relationship at the end of the 90-day listing contract and find somebody who works for a living!

# MINIMUM ADVERTISEMENT

You may be able to negotiate in the listing contract the details of the advertising program that the real estate agent will conduct on your behalf. You're going to pay the real estate agent for selling your home. If the real estate agent is not prepared to advertise your home for sale in the HOMES FOR SALE SECTION of your local newspaper, then something is wrong. Maybe the real estate agent doesn't have the money to advertise your home because he doesn't sell enough homes to afford it and that should indicate to you that you are working with the wrong real estate agent!

# RIGHT TO SELL

Try to negotiate your right to sell the house to any person who is not working with the real estate agent or who is not responding to the real estate agent's advertising. If you sell your own home, why should the real estate agent get a check for your efforts? Thus, you should try to negotiate a listing contract that gives you the right to sell the home directly without having to pay commissions to the real estate agent.

# IMPORTANT FACTS ABOUT LISTING AGREEMENTS

Listing agreements are legally binding contracts which establish the fiduciary (legal) relationship between the owner/seller of real property and the real estate representative selling the real property on behalf of the owner. The only way a listing contract can be terminated is as follows:

1) Sale of the property.

2) Expiration of the contract date indicated in the listing.
   (The expiration date must be specific and in writing.)

3) Mutual agreement between Broker and property Owner to cancel the listing agreement.

4) Destruction of the property (acknowledged by all parties).

5) Bankruptcy and legal loss of property.

6) Death of the property owner.

7) Government changes in zoning and usage of the property.

8) Broker cancellation (May be a breech of contract, obtain legal advice. Broker may be liable for damages.)

9) Owner cancellation (May be a breech of contract, obtain legal advice before breaking a listing agreement. You may be liable for damages.)

# CONCLUSION

Thank you for purchasing "Everything A Real Estate Agent Doesn't Want You To Know." We hope that the information was as helpful as you expected. By following the steps in this book it is possible to save yourself thousands of dollars off the selling price of real estate. Using the principles outlined in the book, people have saved more than $10,000.00 off the selling price of homes they have purchased! Good luck in all you do.

# GLOSSARY OF TERMS

## A

**Abstract of title**—A brief history of a property title. An abstract of title is usually a chronological history of recorded instruments that affect the title of the subject property. In many states an attorney performs a title search using the abstract. The attorney will then issue an opinion which can be used to obtain title insurance.

**Abut**—To connect or join. Two pieces of property which touch each other are said to abut.

**Acceptance**—The act of accepting an offer to enter into a contract. Acceptance is legal and binding when the seller and purchaser agree to the initial terms or after all offers have been made and are deemed acceptable by both parties.

**Accessory building**—A structure detached from but on the same property as a main building. Examples include garages, storage buildings and guest houses.

**Acre**—Land that measures 43,560 square feet. A 200' x 218' lot is 43,600 square feet—just over an acre.

**Addendum**—An agreement or list that is added to a contract or other document such as a letter of intent. The FHA and VA both require that an addendum be added to a sales contract written before the appraisal occurs. Addendums are sometimes referred to as 'amendatory language.'

**Administrator**—A person appointed by an appropriate court of law to settle the estate of a person who died without a will. There are many classifications of administrators serving different specific duties.

**Aesthetic value**—The value of a property attributable to beauty created by both improvements and natural surroundings. A densely wooded lot may add aesthetic value to a property.

**Affidavit**—A written statement sworn to before a notary public or any officer with authority to administer an oath.

**Agency**—The relationship between an agent and a principal. There are both general and specific agencies.

**Agent**—A person authorized to represent or act for another person (the principal) in negotiations with third parties. An agent may be either expressed or implied.

**Appraisal**—An opinion of property value. This is usually a written statement of an appraiser's opinion of value for a specific purpose of a property on a given date.

**Appreciation**—An increase in the value of a property.

**As Is**—Property sold in its present state of condition with no warranties made as to the heating, plumbing, wiring or other factors.

**Assessor**—The individual charged with determining the fair market value of a property for tax purposes.

**Assign**—The act of transferring property or rights to another.

**Assignee**—One who receives property or rights.

## B

**Bilateral contract**—A contract in which each party vows to perform an act in exchange for the other party's promise to perform.

**Blockbusting**—An illegal practice of promoting panic selling in an all-white neighborhood because someone of a minority or ethnic background has moved in or is said to be moving into that same neighborhood. The blockbuster attempts to profit from depressed prices or by gaining listings from panic sellers.

**Board of Realtors®**—The local association of Realtors who belong to the state and national associations of Realtors.

**Breach of contract**—Failure to live up to the terms of a contract. The party who has not breached the contract can rescind the terms of the agreement or can sue for damages.

**Broker**—A properly licensed agent who, for a fee or other consideration, serves as an agent for owners in the process of selling or leasing a property. A broker usually works for a seller who pays a commission.

## C

**Caveat emptor**—Latin phrase meaning 'let the buyer beware.' This doctrine, which holds that a purchaser must thoroughly examine a property to satisfy the condition of its improvements, is diminishing as binding in the eyes of the court system.

**Certificate of completion**—A statement issued by an engineer or architect certifying the completion of a construction project in accordance with the terms of approved plans and specifications.

**Certificate of title**—An attorney's written opinion, based on public records, regarding the status of the title on a given property.

**Chattel**—Personal property that is not permanently attached to a given real estate parcel or structure.

**Clear title**—Title that is marketable and free of any doubts.

**Closing**—The time and ceremony where an actual transfer of title from seller to purchaser occurs. Also called 'settlement.'

**Cloud on title**—An existence of a claim that impairs the owner's case for clear title. A cloud can usually be removed by judicial procedure.

**Comparable**—Properties that are comparable or similar to a subject property. Used for appraisal purposes.

**Comparable sales**—Those sales, usually geographically near, that are used in the market approach to value.

**Concessionary items/concessions**—Items that are paid for or given by a seller to induce a buyer to purchase or lease a property.

**Contract**—A written agreement between two or more parties stating the contract or sale price and the terms and conditions of the sale.

**Convey**—To transfer a property title from one party to another using an acceptable legal instrument.

**Cooperating broker or sale**—A sale in which two or more agents participate.

**Demographics**—Statistical information concerning population growth and trends.

**Description**—The property address and its legal description used for real estate purposes.

**Distressed property**—A property in trouble due to cost overruns, poor management or other conditions affecting the mortgagor's ability to repay a loan on a timely basis.

**Dual contract**—An illegal practice of an agreement between a seller and purchaser that is different from the agreement shown to the lender.

**Duplex**—A dwelling housing two families.

**Earnest money**—A cash deposit accompanying a sales contract used as a show of good faith.

**Economic depreciation**—Loss of property value often caused by changes in the neighborhood or zoning patterns.

**Eminent domain**—The right of government authorities to acquire property by an exercise of its powers of condemnation. The property acquired must be for public use and the owner must be justly compensated.

**Equal Credit Opportunity Act (ECOA)**—A federal law passed in 1975 enacted to prohibit lenders from discriminating on the basis of race, sex, color, religion, national origin, marital status, age or receipt of public assistance.

**Equity**—A value minus indebtedness.

**Eviction**—The legal proceeding a landlord uses to regain possession of a property.

**Evidence of title**—Legal documentation supporting the ownership of a property.

**Exclusive listing**—A written contract to sell property for a specific period of time.

**Execute**—To perform in such a way as to be legally valid and to the standards of a contract.

## F

**Fiduciary**—One who acts in a financial role on behalf of another.

**Foreclosure**—The legal action allowing a mortgagee to sell a property in an attempt to satisfy a mortgagor's debt.

**Forfeiture**—The loss of money or other considerations due to failure to live up to the terms of an agreement.

**Fraud**—The intentional misrepresentation of facts or figures used to deceive another party.

## G-K

**Gross area**—The square footage of a structure as measured by the outside walls.

**Ground lease**—A lease of the ground or land and not the improvements of that land.

**Hidden defect**—A cloud on a title not found by a search of public records.

**Highest and best use**—The ideal use of a property, according to an appraiser and relating to zoning conditions.

**Hold harmless clause**—A contract provision protecting a party from claims.

**Hypothecate**—To pledge property as collateral for a debt without surrendering title or possession of that property.

**Improved land**—Property which has been partially or fully developed, including installation of roads, curbs, utilities and even buildings.

**Improvements**—Additions and items permanently attached to a given property or structure.

**Incompetent**—A person deemed unable to fulfill contractual obligations, perhaps due to mental illness or being a minor.

**Insurable title**—A property of suitable quality for title insurance to be obtained.

**Joint tenancy**—Two or more parties owning a property. In the event of death, the surviving partner inherits the property.

**Judgement**—A court decision that can result in a lien against a property or the garnishment of wages so a creditor can collect a debt.

**Kickback**—Payment, usually illegal, made in return for a referral resulting in business for the payer; the person being referred is generally unaware of the payment.

# L

**Land contract**—A contract where the purchaser is not given title to the property until the full price has been paid. This allows a seller to regain property more easily in case of default by the buyer.

**Land lease**—A lease in which only the ground is rented.

**Landlocked**—A property that does not have access to a public street except through an adjoining lot.

**Landlord**—A lessor who rents property.

**Landmark**—An identfying mark serving to indicate a boundary for a tract of land.

**Latent defect**—A hidden or concealed problem. This is usually known by the seller but cannot be easily seen by a purchaser or appraiser.

**Lease**—A contract involving the payment of rent for a specific period of time.

**Lease-purchase**—A means of purchasing property through gradual payments above the cost of required rental.

**Legal age**—The age at which a person is no longer a minor and can take title to a property. Also known as majority.

**Legal name**—The name used by an individual for business purposes. This is normally a person's full name.

**Lessee**—A party who rents property; a tenant.

**Lessor**—The party who rents a property.

**Listing**—1) A written contract between a principal and an agent; 2) An agreement between a seller and a broker; 3) A property that a broker has for sale.

# M

**Maintenance**—The work required to keep a building in operating condition.

**Marketable title**—Title to a property that is free from defects.

**Market approach to value**—An appraiser's valuation of property based on sales of similar properties.

**Market price**—The amount paid for a property in an actual transaction.

**Market value**—The price which a seller and buyer can agree on with neither being under duress.

**Minor**—A person not of legal age (too young) to purchase or hold title to property.

**Mortgagee**—The lender on a specific property.

**Mortgagor**—The borrower.

**Multi-family housing**—A residential building with more than one dwelling unit.

**Multiple listing**—A joint effort by two or more real estate brokers to sell a listing.

## N-O

**National Association of Realtors® (NAR)**—An organization of over 600,000 member real estate agents.

**Non-owner occupied**—A property which is not occupied by the owner.

**Notarize**—The act of a Notary Public witnessing the authenticity of a signature.

**Notary Public**—A person authorized to authenticate signatures and administer oaths on certain documents, including contracts, deeds and affidavits.

**Null and void**—A reference to something that cannot be legally enforced.

**Offer**—An agreeement to perform in a specific manner in regard to entering a contract for the purchase of property.

**Offer and acceptance**—The ingredients necessary for a valid contract. An agreement on purchase price and other terms.

**Open house**—Showing a listing during specific hours which have been advertised to the public.

**Open listing**—A listing in which a broker or agent does not have exclusive right to sell.

**Oral contract**—An unwritten (spoken) contract. Seldom used in real estate.

**Owner/occupant**—A person who lives in the property he owns.

## P-Q

**Partnership**—A business association of two or more persons.

**Permanent financing**—Long-term (usually referring to ten or more years) mortgage.

**Physical depreciation**—A property's loss in value resulting from wear and tear due to usage or natural elements.

**Plat**—A map of a land area showing precise boundaries and locations of properties.

**Plot plan**—A drawing showing the site and dimensions of improvements on a property.

**Premises**—Land and improvements.

**Property**—The right to possession and disposition of all things subject to ownership.

**Quadruplex**—Four-unit building.

**Quitclaim deed**—A deed conveying the grantor's rights in a property without disclosing the nature of those rights and with no warranties of ownership.

## R

**Ready, willing and able**—The description of a buyer who is legally capable and financially willing to conduct a purchase.

**Real estate**—Land and its permanently attached improvements.

**Real property**—Rights and interests resulting from the ownership of real estate.

**Realtor®**—A registered trade name used by members of the National Association of Realtors.

**Recording**—Making written instruments a part of public record.

**Redlining**—An illegal practice involving lending institutions restricting the number of loans in certain neighborhoods on the basis or race or ethnic background.

**Rider**—An amendment or addendum to a contract.

**Right-of-way**—Similar to an easement, a right-of-way can be the usage of property for a public road or other access route.

## S-V

**Sale-leaseback**—Property that is sold to a buyer who then leases the property back to the seller.

**Subject property**—A property that is the subject of a sale, lease or appraisal.

**Survey**—A drawing denoting measurements and improvements of a parcel of land. Also the process by which the land is measured.

**Title**—Documentation regarding the rightful ownership of a property.

**Title Insurance**—An insurance policy warranting the validity of a property title. It insures against losses arising through any outstanding liens or encumbrances.

**Title search**—Investigation of public records to determine the status of a title.

**Usury**—The act of charging interest rates above those permitted by state law.

**Valuable consideration**—Money or other items that can support a contract.

**Vendor**—A seller.

## W-Z

**Waiver**—To surrender a claim, privilege or right voluntarily.

**Warranty**—A promise guaranteeing the truth of certain statements or facts.

**Zero lot lines**—A structure with one or more sides resting directly on the boundary line of the property on which the building sits.